GOD, WHAT IS MY BABY'S NAME?

SUSAN MARIE PENDER

CHRISTIAN INTERNATIONAL
PUBLISHING SANTA ROSA BEACH,
FLORIDA

GOD, WHAT IS MY BABY'S NAME?
Copyright © 2016 by Susan Marie Pender.
All rights reserved

This book or parts thereof may not be reproduced in any form, stored in a retrieval system, or transmitted in any form by any means—electronic, mechanical, photocopy, recording, or otherwise—without prior written permission of the publisher, except as provided by United States of America copyright law.

Christian International Publishing
177 Apostles Way
Santa Rosa Beach, Florida 32459
www.cipublishing.org

ISBN: 978-0-939868-92-6
Printed in the United States of America

All scripture quotations, unless otherwise indicated, are from the Holy Bible, New International Version. NIV. Copyright 1972, 1978, 1984 by Biblica, Inc. Used by permission of Zondervan. All rights reserved worldwide. www.zondervan.Com

For speaking engagements or questions,

Contact Susan Marie Pender
Susanmariepender@gmail.com
www.lilyofthevalleyhealing.com

Acknowledgments

With a most grateful heart, I want to acknowledge God Almighty as the One who pursued me with His unconditional love and changed the course of my life forever.

I would like to express my gratitude to Christian International founder, Bishop Bill Hamon, for establishing Ministry Training College (MTC) that welcomes people of all ages, cultures, and backgrounds, to study and develop their gifts so they can fulfill their hearts' desires that the Lord Jesus Christ gave them. I am also grateful for the Ministry Training College Directors, Pastors Joe and Ana Bucciero, for the support and guidance they offered me while I have been a student.

I am grateful to Sherry Jensrud for sharing God's love and truth with me.

Finally, I want to thank Martha Kontur for hearing my heart and for editing this book.

Table of Contents

Introduction iii

I Really Want to Have Children 1

Something Has Gone Wrong 3

Inside the Abortion Clinic 9

Depression Sets In 17

God Answers My Question 21

God, What is My Baby's Name? 25

Missionary from Home 31

Women Need the Truth 35

Not Much Emotional Support 39

Is Abortion Found in the Bible? 45

Forgive and Live 53

More From the Author 59

Introduction

My whole life, I dreamed about being a mother one day. I wanted to have children and looked forward to the time when I could experience being pregnant and have a family.

Having an abortion was the farthest thing from my mind. Never a consideration that I entertained, abortion, I believed, was never a right choice.

When my doctor gave me a negative diagnosis about my baby, I was encouraged to have an abortion by the professionals in the medical field, who have strayed far from the ways God meant for us to live. I didn't feel right about abortion and now that I experienced it, I understand why it is so destructive to the baby and the mother.

During this trauma, I needed answers. Where does sickness come from? Why do people suffer? Through it all, God was always good to help me when I cried out to Him.

If you have had an abortion, you can be forgiven and restored. Jesus paid for your sins, and all of your sorrows. Your emotions and your physical body can be healed, just by asking God and receiving His love.

Chapter One

I Really Want to Have Children

I had been married for ten years and was beginning to look at what life would be like without family and children. During our marriage the years passed by quickly. After relocating our home eleven times, I felt the importance of starting a family. My husband didn't want children. I assumed children were a part of being married.

Growing up in a family of five siblings and so many cousins it was difficult to count them all, there was always someone around to talk to, or to play with. We even had our own softball team on any given day. Being raised in this caring environment, a family of my own became very important to me. Not wanting this childless void in my life any longer, I expressed my desires to my husband. In just a short time afterward, I became pregnant.

During my work as a full-time waitress and a student completing nursing school, I became aware of the precious life developing inside of me. I laid my hands on my tummy and talked to my little one. I told him how special he was, I sang to him and thanked God for him. Every day my love for my son grew as I looked forward to this wonderful life. My hopes for having a caring family were developing within me. My dreams were becoming a reality.

Though being pregnant fulfilled my longing for a child, my marriage was not a close, loving one. We did not have the intimacy that I yearned for in a relationship. We did not share mutual thoughts and feelings. My husband worked in the construction industry, which took him long distances away from home for several weeks, leaving me alone much of the time. Our marriage was empty.

Because we relocated so often, I didn't have many good friends. I felt isolated in my own home and eager for new opportunities. When I was invited to my co-worker's home to study the Bible, I knew I was in the right place. Though I gave my life to the Lord several years earlier, God was awakening my heart to know more about Him.

He created us to be loved and appreciated in relationships. Although I was lonely and looking for what would fill the longings in my heart, I had expectations for the life inside of me and new friendships through this Bible study.

Chapter Two

Something Has Gone Wrong

When my baby was at twenty-four weeks gestation the doctor questioned why my abdomen was growing proportionately larger than normal. After my examination, he scheduled an ultrasound with a follow-up office visit two days later to discuss the results. Typically, I went alone to all my doctor visits. I was alone this day as well.

I understood the ultrasound was a standard procedure, so I was not too concerned. The doctor, at this point, had not given any reason to cause me concern. I suspected my baby was just a little bigger than normal, or maybe it had to do with how I carried a child. Everyone is different, I reasoned. I was not prepared for what he was about to tell me.

The doctor informed me that the recent ultrasound showed my baby was hydrocephalic. This medical diagnosis indicates abnormal accumulation of fluid in cerebral ventricles, causing the skull to enlarge. The compression destroys much of the neural tissue in the brain. My baby's hydrocephalic condition was extensive. The doctor explained that at this point the pressure on the baby's brain caused him discomfort, and there would be some brain damage. The doctor

God, What is My Baby's Name?

advised me to have an abortion as soon as it could be scheduled.

I told him I didn't believe having an abortion was the right solution for me. He argued that since my health was in danger, it was a proper solution. The doctor then reiterated that when the mother's health was in danger an abortion was proper protocol.

He scheduled the abortion procedure for me at Ramsey Hospital in St. Paul the following week. The next day I was to discuss the situation with my husband when he returned from his work out of state.

Crying as I drove home from my appointment that day, I thought, "This doctor wants me to get rid of my baby, just because there is something wrong with him!"

I desperately wanted my baby to have the chance to live. Not wanting to end my pregnancy, I struggled with the decision of ending his life. I felt an overwhelming love for my baby and I desperately wanted to have him. The situation seemed ironic. I was being encouraged to choose to destroy someone I loved just because there was something wrong with him.

In today's society, we have the medical capabilities to detect various health issues, giving us choices as to how we want to deal with them. This choice of abortion didn't seem right to me. The thought that my little one inside of me did not have a chance to live, was difficult to comprehend.

"This will be the only time that I will have to talk to him. I am never going to hear his voice or look into his eyes," I thought desperately to myself, "Where is this God that I have come to know? Where is He when I'm hurting? Where is God when my baby is having problems growing? How does God feel about my baby's difficulty, and about abortion? Does God know or hear me when I cry out to Him for help? Does God want to do anything to help me? Why does God seem so far away from me now?"

When I shared the diagnosis with my husband, he suggested we do as the doctor advised. That was all that we discussed – that was all that was said – that was all that was mentioned - that was all. Why was this a surprise to me? He never cared about me on any other day. There was no one who cared about my life.

I tried to reach my parents for hope, but they were on an overseas trip. I had no one else in my life who I could talk to about this situation. Keeping my thoughts and feelings inside, I did not even share my situation with the Bible study group. I felt it was too personal.

However, we are not meant to be isolated from others. People are meant to live in relationships and to express themselves freely.

I looked to my husband and family for help but no one seemed to understand my heart.

God, What is My Baby's Name?

Since I lived a long distance away, my relatives did not stay in touch with me regularly. My extended family seemed to be dealing with many unresolved issues in their own lives and never were a source of help for me in the past. Based on the difficult situations and circumstances they were experiencing, I felt they were not capable of giving good advice.

Growing up in my family, abortion was never discussed. I had never heard it talked about in my church. It surely wasn't an option that my parents would have chosen for any of their children. I never thought I would be confronted with this choice. I would never choose to destroy a life inside of me. Yet now, I felt I was forced to make this choice, because of the evidence that revealed my baby's defect.

The doctor told me I was in danger. He informed me that simply the state of pregnancy puts a mother at risk. However, I always believed being pregnant was a normal condition. Never thinking I was in danger, I was not concerned about myself. I remained healthy. Not having any abnormal symptoms such as high blood pressure or abnormal sugar levels, I felt healthy in every way. I knew that pregnancy was a normal process for mothers. This was how God intended for us to have children. Surely, God did not intend for a mother to be at risk by becoming pregnant. When a baby is having difficulty within the womb, medical protocol labels

Something Has Gone Wrong

the mother's life at risk. In my case, I felt this was not true. I had no symptoms of distress. Not realizing prayer was an option at this time in my life, I did not know I could ask God to heal my baby. I hadn't yet come to understand the healing aspect of God.

Later, I would read about people who prayed when faced with these kinds of situations, and sometimes they saw their circumstance turn around, and their babies were healed. Some of their stories were about babies in the womb who were also diagnosed with hydrocephalic conditions. After prayer, they no longer had this defect. God wants to heal us today, but I was not aware of that at the time.

During my appointment, my doctor never presented me any other medical options or asked me what I wanted to do. He never inquired about any emotional struggle I might be experiencing. My husband never asked me how I felt about having an abortion in a city three hundred miles away from home. I felt like I was all alone.

No one asked me how I struggled with having my baby aborted. No one discussed what was best for me emotionally. Having the birth at a local hospital was never encouraged. No option to monitor the progression of the baby's development during the pregnancy was offered.

Daily I identified with this real life that was inside of me. People all around me were making decisions on what should be done concerning my baby, which

God, What is My Baby's Name?

conflicted with my own heart. I was all alone feeling as if I had no choices. In my desperation, I agreed to abort my baby.

I arranged to take off the next week from my job. I was experiencing a state of shock. Methodically, I began packing a suitcase. Everything happened too quickly.

One day, I went in for a routine appointment and now within a day I would be traveling to a city three hundred miles away to have them remove, from me, the most precious gift I had ever been given.

Chapter Three

Inside the Abortion Clinic

As scheduled, I walked up to the doors to enter the abortion clinic, wondering why there were no protesters standing outside trying to stop me. I thought it was strange that there was no one there to tell me I was making a mistake. Already prepared in my mind what I would say to them, I imagined telling them I had no other choice. Perhaps I was looking for someone to support the negative feelings I was wrestling with about this decision.

I found the waiting room and registered, there I waited to see a doctor. They told me they would be keeping my baby at the hospital after the delivery. To determine whether the hydrocephalic condition was hereditary, they were going to perform some genetic testing on the baby. This seemed medically appropriate to me, but at the same time I didn't understand the heartache and pain it would cause me. After the abortion, I assumed I would still be taking my baby home at some point for his burial. Because of my anxiety, my sole focus was on the abortion itself; I could not reason beyond that.

As I sat in the office filling out my personal information sheets, I couldn't help noticing the other

God, What is My Baby's Name?

young women who were in the waiting room with me. They were filling out their forms held by a clipboard.

A nurse was seated behind a desk. There were no men there except for my husband. There was no one who appeared to be a parent or even of that age. We all waited, silently, for our names to be called to see the doctor. No one was smiling or happy. No one talked. No one seemed consciously aware of anyone else.

Robotically, each woman with head down, concentrated alone in her thoughts. Time seemed to stand still. There were no feelings or emotions expressed by anyone there, just solemn faces. I will never forget how numb everyone appeared.

Crying desperately within myself I screamed silently, "I don't want to be here. I want my baby! Maybe these mothers want to get rid of their babies, but I want mine. I love my baby."

I continued grieving in my thoughts, "I've been singing to my baby, and talking to him every day. I want to keep my baby." No one could hear the tortured voice inside of me. I continued to fill out my personal information sheet.

The nurse receptionist called my name. In a professional manner, she asked me to come with her. We walked quietly down the hall to the doctor's office. The nurse led me to a large room with several

Inside the Abortion Clinic

hospital beds and asked me to sit in a chair by a desk. She pulled a curtain around us, separating me from the others.

As the doctor interviewed me, I began to understand more about my circumstance. Since the doctor had all of my records, he informed me that my gynecologist was his good friend. He had actually completed his internship at this facility. I understood. This was one of the reasons why I was sent here, so far from home.

Evidently, my gynecologist was very familiar with abortions as a remedy for pregnancy. My doctors were educated and trained to accept abortion as the answer to alleviate complications.

"Are you okay with this decision?" the doctor continued the interview.

I replied hesitantly, "Yes."

In truth, I wasn't okay. I thought I had no other option. He repeatedly asked me this question, but I was not okay with having an abortion.

The doctor explained that he would be inserting Laminar during this visit, which would assist in dilation to prepare me for the delivery tomorrow. He advised me again that I would not be able to change my mind after this.

He instructed me to return the next day, when they would give me an intravenous medication to induce contractions allowing me to have my baby. Over and over again, the doctor asked if I was sure I wanted to

God, What is My Baby's Name?

have the procedure. Reiterating that after this point I could not change my mind. I was unsettled inside.

His repetition came as a flashing, warning sign to me as he said, "You cannot change your mind."

Thoughts were surging through my brain. "There must be something really wrong or evil on the other side of this. They must know more than I know - they have seen things that I am not aware of. Didn't he know I was here on my doctor's advice? I didn't have another option."

Does the reason someone has an abortion determine if it is right or wrong? If an abortion is advised by a doctor, does that make it a right choice?

I thought it was right to comply with my doctor's advice. I assumed he had my best interest, health, and welfare in mind, even though my conscience was not in agreement with the abortion.

I trusted my doctor's advice. Surely there were other women who were here before me, who weren't sure they wanted to go through with their procedure. They too, must have felt that an abortion was their only option. Maybe they were intimidated to come here.

I was sure there were women who desperately wanted to back out, but they were paralyzed when the doctor said, "You cannot change your mind after this."

That night my baby moved inside of me. It would

be the last time I would feel him move. My emotions overwhelmed me with sadness. His wonderful life inside of me would not be there tomorrow.

The tomorrow arrived and we went to Ramsey Hospital where the nurse helped me to my bed. She started an intravenous fluid, Pitocin, which caused contractions to begin. An hour later, I delivered my baby. He did not make a sound. I was relieved and saddened at the same time.

My baby looked normal in every way. He was a perfectly formed little boy. I held him in my arms wrapped in a cloth sheet. He was beautiful in every way, except there was no breath in him.

I held him for only a few minutes, and then a nurse said she had to take him. I hadn't thought to bring a baby blanket to wrap him in. I hadn't thought about what I wanted to say to him when I saw him. I wasn't prepared for the moments of holding him, and then letting someone take him, not ever being able to have him back, ever again.

A nurse rolled my cot-type bed, to a large room, where everyone and everything was divided by curtains. Preparing me for a curettage, the doctor would remove the placenta by scraping my uterine wall. After giving me Demerol for pain, the nurse gave me intravenous valium to relax me during this procedure.

The Demerol was not effective. I felt every horrible scraping that his medical tools made inside of me. I

God, What is My Baby's Name?

felt every movement of the doctor's hands.

The nurse stood at my right side, holding my hand. My eyes were open during this procedure. I tried to cry out to the nurse with my eyes staring at her, as I was unable to communicate verbally. I was unable to move any facial muscles. I was unable to make a sound.

My eyes were open, but I was unable to tell them about the terrific pain I was having. The valium I was given made me appear relaxed and numb though I squeezed the nurse's hand as tight as I could. The pain was extreme during the doctor's curettage procedure.

Staring at the nurse the entire time, I desperately wanted to tell her to make the doctor stop. The pain was unbearable. Though she saw terrible agony in my eyes, there was no verbal communication between us. I was desperately helpless and alone.

A little later, I dressed myself and left. As my husband and I began our four-hour drive, I realized that we didn't take our baby home. We never even discussed with the clinic about taking him home for a funeral. They could have done the genetic testing, and we still could have taken him home to have a proper burial. However, we weren't even given the option. The conversation never came up.

Because of the trauma of the abortion, we, or I didn't think to ask if we would be taking our baby

Inside the Abortion Clinic

home with us. In fact, the doctor never mentioned it. I realized this whole abortion industry was horribly wrong! It had to be the most evil place on earth!

God, What is My Baby's Name?

Chapter Four

Depression Sets In

Immediately, life resumed. Within a few days, I returned to my place of work as a surgical nurse in a nearby hospital. My husband returned to his job in another state, leaving me alone for weeks at a time.

I became severely depressed. I could function at my job, but when I was home alone, I cried most of the time. During this period, thoughts rushing through my mind tormented me. I wanted to know where my baby was now. We just left him there, at the hospital. Even though he was not living, I still felt a bonding for my child and a sense of responsibility to care for his lifeless body in a humane fashion.

I was anxious to know how my baby felt about the choice I made to end his life. I had been telling my baby that I loved him and that I was going to take care of him, but then it was over. It had all come to an end.

Could God really see me, and know the horrible pain I was feeling? Deeper depression washed over me. I had no hope; I could not get through it. The weight of guilt for ending my baby's life was overwhelming. Feeling all alone in the world, I had little desire to live. This deep depression continued.

God, What is My Baby's Name?

I knew abortion was a wrong choice. I knew it deep inside of me. God designed us to feel guilty for our sins by giving us a conscience. A level of guilt is appropriate for sin. I knew it in my heart. Repenting to God, I laid on my floor crying. Yet, the pain inside my heart remained.

Many evenings, day after day, I lay on my living room floor, and cried until there were no more sounds, no more moans. Yearning for someone to appear at the door of my house, I hoped for comfort. No one came. No one knew I was in overwhelming emotional pain. This grief continued for months. Out of exhaustion, I finally gave up on God, telling him I could no longer have a relationship with Him.

With no more strength to cry, I entered into a superficial-functioning in my life. I was alive, but my emotions were numb. All excitement and reason for living was drained from me. I had exhausted my emotional strength.

In desperation, I sought counseling. If I could talk to someone about my loss, and guilt, I reasoned I might return to my normal self. I went through a trauma that stole innocence from me. How could it be restored?

It was during the second therapy session that my counselor suggested I find a male companion. Since my husband was away so much, he reasoned that my needs were not being fulfilled. Even if I did not have a good marriage. I was still married. Though I was in emotional turmoil, I had more common sense than this counselor. My hope for professional help ended that day.

Through my trauma, I continued working as a nurse at my community hospital. Doing the best I could, I proceeded with my routine of life. Struggling with depression, and questions, my pain remained.

God, What is My Baby's Name?

Chapter Five

God Answers My Question

One day while I was at work, my friend invited me to return to the Bible study at her home. I told her about the abortion; how I had waited so long to have a baby, and the outcome was not at all what I expected. I loved him so much and lost him so quickly. I wanted answers but didn't know who could help me find them.

I shared my confusion about who God was during this time, and I could not serve Him if He gave life, then let it be taken away. My friend, sensitive to my honest feelings, suggested I read John 10:10.

The thief comes only to steal and kill and destroy, I have come that they may have life, and have it to the full.
John 10:10, NIV

Excited inside after reading this scripture, I felt in my heart that this was what I was looking for. All of my questions were answered in this scripture.

Instantly, I felt joy leap inside of me for the first time in a year. God spoke to me, through scripture, and through other people. Deep inside, I knew God was not responsible for my baby dying. I knew I had made the decision that ended my baby's life that day. I didn't understand where the sickness came from, what caused it or why, but I knew that God could not be the author of sickness if He is the author of life.

Thanking God for this scripture, I knew in my heart the development of my baby and the abortion were not God's fault. Telling Him over and over, I repented. I was sorry for the abortion. I was sorry for turning away from God during my pain and confusion.

The months of crying out to God on my living room floor were my time of grieving over my baby. I knew I made a wrong choice even though my mind did not understand everything about it. I began to deeply question the horrible nature of the abortion industry.

Understanding more and more about the darkness of abortion, I realized its negative effects on me. This act caused a crushing grief in my heart over my loss, and overwhelming guilt of choosing to end my baby's life in that horrible environment.

During my initial visit with the doctor at Ramsey Hospital, he told me that I was already dilated to two centimeters. I realized that my body was responding normally to my baby's hydrocephalic condition. As a natural response, my body would have gone into labor early. I could have birthed my baby normally at my home, or hospital, providing a caring, and loving environment.

Neither doctor offered this option to me. Birthing my baby naturally would have lessened my grieving and pain. I would have mourned the loss of my baby, but I would not have suffered the guilt of choosing to end his life.

I will never forget the cold, solemn environment with the mothers sitting silently waiting for their names to be called. Abortion is not a remedy for pregnancy or its complications. The effect of abortion on women is different than the effects of rape, incest, or miscarriage. Rape and incest are sexual abuse. The woman knows that she was violated and victimized. Even if she cooperated after a pattern of abuse continued, she still knows she is being victimized.

When a woman has an abortion, she knows it was her decision. Even if others encouraged her, it was her choice to say yes. Though a woman still grieves the loss of her baby when she has a miscarriage, she knows it was not her fault. It was not a choice she made.

When a woman makes the choice of abortion there is a deep sense of guilt ignited within her soul. She may go into denial, feeling like she did nothing wrong, but it is just a coping mechanism for the pain of guilt and loss.

Women are given a natural God-given instinct to mother, care for, and to nourish the life living and growing within her. When she chooses to destroy this life, she is destroying a part of her conscience, a part of her own life. She violates her own self. There is a heavy load of guilt that comes upon any woman who has an abortion. If they are unable to deal with their

God, What is My Baby's Name?

feelings and emotions because the pain is so great, they will deny them and bury them deep inside.

I was very grateful that God used my friend as His voice to bring me the answer, unlocking my guilt and emotional pain. A sense of freedom and joy replaced the burden of guilt I was carrying. God heard me calling out to him. God set up a way to get His answer to me. I was more able to move on with my life. Feeling loved in a way I had never felt before, I realized I was not alone. Even when I was by myself, I was not alone. God truly loved me and was with me.

Chapter Six

God, What is My Baby's Name?

Several months after I returned to work at the hospital in Crookston, a woman was admitted for premature labor. She was at the exact gestation that I was when my baby was born; twenty-four weeks. Though it is possible, it is not likely that a baby will live at this age. The emotion of grief filled me as I identified with this woman.

I heard from the other nurses that a chaplain was brought to her room to baptize her baby as soon as it was delivered. The new parents were prepared because the baby was not expected to live. In order for their baby to enter Heaven, they believed he must be water baptized. I wondered. Where was my baby spending eternity?

Many denominations support the belief that a person is saved and able to enter Heaven only if they are baptized. They may believe that a person is saved by grace through faith, but many still uphold infant baptism because of tradition. Essentially, they believe their infant's baptism assures his or her salvation. With the sprinkling of water on the head, the pastor or priest prays over the child and declares that their soul belongs to God.

My parents raised my siblings and me with the same doctrinal belief. We were all baptized as infants. When anyone in our church attended funerals, our pastor would assure the family of their loved one's salvation, because of their infant baptism.

Later in life I came to know this gave a false sense of eternal security. Infant baptism did not provide a way for me to know God personally. Making a personal choice to receive Jesus Christ as my savior ensured my eternal security.

I received the person, Jesus Christ, into my life when I was twenty-three years old. Until that time, I never knew Him as my personal savior. Recognizing the sin in my life, I asked Jesus Christ to be my Savior and Redeemer. After this, I attended a church that baptized by full immersion for those who had decided to receive Jesus Christ into their lives.

Scriptures confirm that after we believe and confess Jesus Christ as our Lord and Savior we are to be baptized. As we are immersed in the water of baptism, it symbolizes dying with Jesus on the cross. As we come up from the water, it symbolizes a resurrection of new life, just as Jesus was resurrected. This is how we know we have eternal life. Here's what scripture says.

> *I write these things to you who believe in the name of the Son of God so that you may know that you have eternal life.*
> 1 John 5:13, NIV

God, What is My Baby's Name?

> *Whoever believes and is baptized will be saved, but whoever does not believe will be condemned.*
> Mark 16:16, NIV

To be saved you only need to receive Jesus Christ as your Savior. I knew salvation did not depend on infant baptism, but this mother, whose baby was not going to live, was comforted with the baptism of her baby. She did all that she felt in her heart was right, bringing her comfort in a time of tragedy. None the less, this emergency situation caused me to consider my baby once again. Where is he? What might he be doing right now?

During my quiet time at home, I talked to God about him. Looking at scriptures on baptism, I hoped to comfort myself. It was then that I realized we had not given our baby a name.

One evening I asked my husband if he wanted to name our baby. He was not interested. Furthermore, he did not want to talk about the situation ever again. His response made me grateful to have a personal relationship with God, especially during this time. He was the only person I talked to about things on my heart.

I was not satisfied without a name for my baby boy. When it was dark and quiet, I lay on my bed alone. I discussed it with God.

God, What is My Baby's Name?

"I believe my baby is in Heaven with You, and I know that You must already be calling him by a name there. You wouldn't just refer to him as nothing, or as no-name, or as baby. I didn't have a name picked out for him while I was pregnant, nor did I give him a name after he was born. So after these months, You must be calling my baby something. If You, God, are in Heaven, and my baby is in Heaven, then You would know my baby's name."

It just made more sense for me to ask God what they were calling my baby. When I asked God what my baby's name was, I heard a still small voice inside of me say, "Marcus."

I replied, "Oh, Mark. That's a very nice name."

God responded lovingly, "No, I said, Marcus."

God wanted to make sure I understood his correct name. I pondered the name Marcus for a moment. Happily, I thought, I could not have picked out a better name.

Scripture says God calls us by our name while we are still in the womb. Isaiah 43:1 says, "But now, this is what the LORD says -- he who created you, Jacob, he who formed you, Israel, Do not fear, for I have redeemed you, I have summoned you by name, you are mine."

Jeremiah 1:5 says, "Before I formed you in the womb I knew you, before you were born I set you

apart, I appointed you as a prophet to the nations."
God forms us in the womb, and He knows us. God is the one that calls us by our name.

Lying quietly on my bed that evening, I experienced a precious stillness and peace in my room. I heard God's voice speak my baby's name. I did not have any name picked out during my pregnancy. Because my husband and I never once discussed a name, I did not have any preconceived ideas.

God clearly spoke my baby's name to me. This reveals the heart of God as a Father. He knew my baby's name while he was formed in the womb. He is a loving and kind Father. Another name for God is Abba, as we see in Romans.

> *So you have not received a spirit that makes you fearful slaves. Instead, you received God's Spirit when he adopted you as his own children.[a] Now we call him, "Abba, Father.*
> Romans 8:15, NLT

God is a Father and He knows every one's name. God gives a name to every baby who comes to Heaven without a name. Life begins at conception with the union of the man's sperm and the woman's egg. Every baby who is aborted, yet considered only *tissue,* was a living being.

When this baby is removed from the mother's

God, What is My Baby's Name?

womb, God receives the baby into Heaven and gives the baby a name. When God kindly spoke to me and answered my heartfelt question, He was restoring my soul. He was removing my grief. He was healing me of my emotional pain.

Chapter Seven

Missionary from Home

John 10:10 tells us the thief wants to kill, steal, and destroy our lives. God wills for us to live life fully, without sickness. The thief steals health from us and destroys people's lives. Jesus came to give us life in every area.

In the home Bible study, I was attending, I learned about praying for others. I learned that we can pray for people who are sick, to be well, and pray for those who don't know Christ as their savior, to come to this knowledge. This is somewhat like standing in the gap for another person and pleading their case for them like an attorney would in a courtroom.

Praying for others became a way of life for me that was fulfilling. I wanted to help other people come to know this loving God that I was discovering. Wanting to see people's lives healed, I prayed for them, bringing their situations before God, and asking Him to help them. We can carry each other's burdens.

Carry each other's burdens, and in this way you will fulfill the law of Christ.
Galatian 6:2, NIV

This was a way I could carry another person's

God, What is My Baby's Name?

burden, and hopefully they would turn to our Father, who loved them. My life with Jesus was like being a missionary without having to leave home.

I began spending time praying in my room for my family, and for other people. Playing my guitar, and singing love songs to God, I knew He heard me. I knew he saw me. Feeling so close to Him, I knew He enjoyed drawing me close as well. An overwhelming desire to pray for others gave me a sense of gratification while being in His presence.

On the other hand, I knew the devil would be happy if I stayed away from God. I knew there was a kingdom of darkness that steals, kills, and destroys. By faith I could ask God to intervene on behalf of others, and through prayer remove some of the darkness that was around people and bring damage to the devil's kingdom. I began to understand Matthew 10:39.

> *Whoever finds their life will lose it, and whoever loses their life for my sake will find it.*
> Matthew 10:39, NIV

Choosing to lose my life, I spent my time praying for others and worshipping instead of doing other things. It was more beneficial to be in love with this Jesus, my Savior. Spending my time getting to know Him was more important than pursuing anything else.

Missionary from Home

I was damaging the kingdom of darkness, by being close to the one who loved me most. This was how I was living, knowing and loving God. Having very few material things, I had everything. During these times, I told God that I would go anywhere with Him. I would say anything. I would do anything He asked of me.

For the next ten years, with great joy, I gave my life away praying for others, and worshipping God. I understood, John 15:13.

> *Greater love has no one than this, to lay down one's life for one's friends.*
> John 15:13, NIV

This was the only way I knew how to turn around something that was meant for bad - the loss of my baby and make it good - living a life praying for others.

God, What is My Baby's Name?

Chapter Eight

Women Need the Truth

As time went on, I birthed three more children. One particular day, I was outside in our yard playing with them. I heard the Lord tell me that I should write out my story about abortion. He was so clear that I went into the house and easily began writing out my story.

A couple days later, I received a call from a church I attended occasionally. A woman asked if I had a message God wanted me to share.

I said, "Well, yes I do."

I had no idea how she knew about my message. I had not told anyone. Reasoning that if God had told me to write this out, He probably spoke to this woman about my message. God knows everything. I shared my story the following Sunday night.

A couple weeks later, I got another phone call from someone who wanted me to share at their woman's group. When the day came, I was getting ready to go to their rural church. I was pretty excited to share my story again. By relating my experience, people would become more aware that abortion was not a good choice.

The women from this rural church were homemakers who knew how to sew, grow gardens, and can

God, What is My Baby's Name?

their own foods. I considered them to be wise women. I have to admit that I was a little excited inside about getting to be the speaker to these honored women. I shared my story and my daughter and I sang a song. Even though I was quite inexperienced, the ministry went well. I smiled and just did the best I could.

When I got home I stepped into my bedroom to change my clothes. I wore a rose-colored long dress that I had bought at a used clothing store, but it still looked pretty new. As I was unbuttoning the back of the dress, I realized, I had put my dress on backwards! The buttons should have been in the front of the dress. The neckline was a little higher in the front, and it was now obvious to me that the higher neckline should have been in the back.

Oh my goodness! I just realized that I wore my dress backwards to this women's meeting where, I was the guest speaker! I began to laugh at myself. I could hear God laughing too. God could have told me about this backwards dress before I left my house, but He let me go anyway. He let me see my mistake after I got home.

I thought I was special because I was invited to speak, but then I saw I was not even able to dress myself properly! These women knew how to sew clothes, and could easily identify something odd about my dress. I was sure they must have taken a few second looks at me. My pretty rose colored dress with the high neck in front, and the buttons in the back. I had a good laugh at myself, and God did too. It was worth it!

God let me know that I needed Him in every situation - even in dressing myself. Tenderly, He adjusts our wrong attitudes and character! I wanted to share the truth about abortion to women, and through each experience, my message was heard.

God, What is My Baby's Name?

Chapter Nine
Not Much Emotional Support

On several occasions, I was invited to share my abortion experience. One place was at a church in my hometown, and I stayed at my parent's house. I went there after the service ended. Instead of affirmation about the meeting, we had a discussion about my message that evening.

My mother disagreed with my statement, "Everything in the Bible is the true Word of God."

She questioned how Matthew, Mark, Luke, and John shared some of their experiences with Jesus a little differently in the gospels. Therefore, she dismissed them as unsubstantial.

She went on to explain that in the book of Matthew, the Bible talks about one of the disciples seeing one angel at a certain place, and in the book of Luke, the Bible says another disciple saw two angels at the same place instead of one. Because she felt these related passages contradicted each other, she decided the Bible could not be true.

I didn't know what to say. I was surprised she expressed these feelings to me. At the same time, I was disappointed that she didn't think the Bible was true. I waited to reply to her until the next morning.

As I got ready for bed, I asked God what I was supposed to say to my mom. He reminded me of the time, a few years earlier when I shared with my dad that I loved him and I asked him to stop drinking. I told my parents how I had seen an angel as I spoke to him. My sister was there and witnessed the emotional love that came over my dad that day, which forever changed his life. I never asked my sister if she saw the same angel. If I did, she may have said she saw two or three angels in the room with us that day. The number of angles would not make what God did for my dad that day irrelevant. I was relieved that God answered me so quickly.

In the morning I replied to my mom's question from the night before. I reminded her of the time a few years earlier when I shared with my dad. I related what God showed me about the angels. I continued to explain that we should not discount the encounter my dad experienced just because we did not agree on what each of us saw.

This was the only topic my mother talked about concerning my message, but God gave me understanding. Throughout this discussion, my mother never acknowledged my ministry on abortion. When I did not receive encouragement to speak up for what I knew was right, I felt unsupported and emotionally abandoned.

I experienced a conflict between what my family believed and what I believed to be true. It was as if a piece of the foundation of my family identity was no

Not Much Emotional Support

longer a part of me. I was standing alone on the foundation of my new identity in Christ. My mom never talked to me about the abortion again.

My sister came to visit the next day. Sitting at the table having breakfast she abruptly declared that I did the right thing by having an abortion. Because my baby was hydrocephalic, she believed he would have been a burden to me. Quickly, I disagreed. I told her that ending my baby's life through abortion was not a good decision. I should have sought out prayer for my baby to be healed as I had heard stories of other babies being healed of this condition.

I further explained that my body was not in any danger carrying my baby. I was hurried into making a decision to have him removed from me. This was the first opportunity I had to talk with my sister about the things that happened. I told her we were not even given the option to bring our baby home for a funeral.

There was no more discussion. Though she thought she was supporting me in the abortion, we did not agree at all. My sister did not have any reply. We never discussed it again.

This same day, during a family gathering in the evening, my sister-in-law confronted me about sharing my experience of abortion with others. Standing face to face with me, my back against a wall, angrily, she told me I had no right to tell other women that they should not have an abortion. I explained to her, I was not telling other women what they should do, but I was only sharing my own experience. She continued her argument.

She believed women could do whatever they want with their bodies, and I had no right to speak up like this. Standing alone during this confrontation, I did not receive any support from my family.

I was confused why sharing this difficult time in my life along with the excitement of how God brought me through it, would cause such an upheaval with those around me. I was quickly discovering that I would not be supported by those close to me in sharing this message. I was not condemning anyone or telling anyone what they should do. My only motive was to share the truth of my experience. I wanted to bring the knowledge of the devastation of depression that comes to the mother after having an abortion and that God's forgiveness can restore them. I was standing in this place alone, physically and emotionally.

Though there was no support from my family, I could talk to the women in my Tuesday evening Bible class and God. My heart in sharing my experience was to encourage other people that no matter what difficulties they may be facing, God loves them and He cares for them.

He will be there to help them like He was there for me. Had it not been for God revealing Himself to me, and letting me feel His presence when I was so

Not Much Emotional Support

broken- hearted, I may have ended my own life in deep despair. Though I felt I was standing alone in my family, feeling unloved, I knew God supported me, and this caused me to remain true to what I believed.

God, What is My Baby's Name?

Chapter Ten

Is Abortion Found in the Bible?

When we sin, we open ourselves up to the fruit of that sin. It is called the law of sowing and reaping. Whatever type of seed we put into the ground, determines the type of crop we will grow and harvest. Words and actions are seeds that grow. If we say encouraging words and show kindness to people, they will have hope and more likely feel they can succeed. Speaking negative words to people will cause them to feel sad and less likely to accomplish a goal. Choices we make in our lives will mostly determine how we live. I'm going somewhere with the law of sowing and reaping.

I began to look in the Bible to see if there were any scriptures that talked about abortion. I heard the unusual name Molech mentioned in the Bible. This name referred to the sacrifice of babies and children to this god. I found the scripture in Leviticus.

> *Do not give any of your children to be sacrificed to Molek, for you must not profane the name of your God. I am the Lord.*
> Leviticus 18:21, NIV

This says when we choose to take our children's

God, What is My Baby's Name?

lives or have them removed from the womb so they cannot live, it is the same as offering them to the god called Molek or Molech. God is saying we are not to do this. The prophet Jeremiah refers to this.

They built high places for Baal in the Valley of Ben Hinnom to sacrifice their sons and daughters to Molek, though I never commanded, nor did it enter my mind, that they should do such a detestable thing, and so make Judah si.
Jeremiah 32:35, NIV

What kind of a god would have you kill your son or daughter? It is called an abomination. It is something that God hates. God plans out and maps out our lives before we are born. He has a destiny for each and every one of us. It is not God's purposes to have us destroy lives by aborting them before they are born.

Another scripture in Leviticus refers to Molek and abortion.

The Lord said to Moses, Say to the Israelites, Any Israelite or any foreigner residing in Israel who sacrifices any of his children to Molek is to be put to death. The members of the community are to stone him.' I myself will set my face against him and will cut him off from his people, for by sacrificing his

Is Abortion Found in the Bible?

> *children to Molek he has defiled my sanctuary and profaned My holy name. If the members of the community close their eyes when that man sacrifices one of his children to Molek and if they fail to put him to death, I myself will set my face against him and against his family, and will cut them off from their people together with all who follow him in prostituting themselves to Molek.*
> Leviticus 20:1-6, NIV

These were the commandments that God gave to Moses for the people. They were to live by these commandments. We are not to kill one another. We are not supposed to kill our seed within us.

Let's see what Deuteronomy says,

> *You must not worship the Lord your God in that way, because in worshiping their gods, they do all kinds of detestable things the Lord hates, they even burn their sons and their daughters in the fire as sacrifices to their gods.*
> Deuteronomy 12:31, NIV

Abortion is the destruction of a life. It is murder. The Bible is clear about murder.

> *Thou shalt not murder.*
> Exodus 20:13, NIV

God, What is My Baby's Name?

When we murder someone, we open ourselves up to a spirit of death. That is why women become depressed after having an abortion. A spirit of death has been given an open door to their lives.

As a way of coping with emotional feelings of despair, a woman who has had an abortion may deny any wrongdoing. The feelings may be so painful; they ignore them by burying them. However, these painful emotions of depression will still surface at some time in their lives as anger or bitterness until they are acknowledged.

Women are not prepared for the devastation they experience after abortion. Pro-abortion counseling is wrapped up in lies. Women are told that they need to get rid of the *tissue*. It is not called a baby; it is referred to as *tissue*. You do not need to have a funeral for *tissue*. That is why a funeral is never considered at an abortion clinic, no matter what gestational period the baby is in.

During pregnancy, a woman's body is nourishing a life inside of her. When an abortion removes this life from the womb, the woman's body does not know what to do because all her bodily functions were focused on maintaining life within her.

Causing trauma to all the systems of her body, abortion affects the woman emotionally, physically, spiritually, and mentally. When she returns home to the routine of life; however, she has no understanding of the hormonal changes her body experiences due to the abrupt loss of pregnancy.

The prophet Isaiah speaks what God says,

Can a mother forget the baby at her breast and have no compassion on the child she has borne? Though she may forget, I will not forget you! See I have engraved you on the palms of my hands, your walls are ever before me.
Isaiah 49:15, 16, NIV

God designed our bodies to be life-giving. Our identity is written on God's hands. When we decide to terminate a life inside of us, it contradicts the purpose for our physical body. Interrupting God's design for a mother, it causes her to experience trauma within her body functions. We see this in Leviticus.

For the life of the creature is in the blood.
Leviticus 17:11a, NIV

The cells and the blood of our body work together to provide the best conditions for the correct functioning of all the cells, tissues, and organs of our whole body. During pregnancy, this synopsis includes the child's life within her body. When part of this life-giving process is removed, the life functioning process is interrupted. Health complications are common.

God, What is My Baby's Name?

Related risks caused by abortion include pelvic infections, fever, blood clots in the uterus, heavy bleeding, cut or torn cervix, puncture or tears of the uterine wall, scar tissue, risks in future pregnancies, difficulty breathing, and chest pain.

Some of the psychological and emotional reactions to abortion include depression, anger, fear of disclosure, increased alcohol and drug abuse, nightmares, sexual dysfunction, emotional coldness, eating disorders, anxiety, acute feelings of grief, flashbacks to the abortion procedure, anniversary syndrome, shame and guilt, repeat abortions, fear of judgment, and finally suicide.

My baby was not surgically removed; it was an induced delivery. Therefore, I was not exposed to some of the risks mentioned above. Yet none of these risks were discussed with me before I had my baby at an abortion clinic. I was left to deal with and experience my emotional pain alone without the closure of his death.

After leaving the abortion clinic, the mother does not have any idea what happened to her dead baby. Most have no incentive to find out. Even if she wanted to pursue the issue, it would be difficult to get an answer. She will never know if her unborn baby was thrown in the garbage, incinerated, taken by a medical waste company, or used for scientific research.

When someone dies, a funeral or a ceremony

helps the ones close to the deceased person to mourn. The grieving process has necessary steps to go through. The final gathering of family to support and grieve together over the loss of a life is healthy, mentally and emotionally. With no body or remains of the person, bringing closure to the trauma is difficult.

The Bible recounts abortions throughout history. God's heart for the mothers and babies is for good. The sin of abortion opens doors in the mother's life to depression, murder, violence, anger, or hate. Often bitterness, suicide, idolatry, fear, death, immorality, perversion or pre-mature death can be a result from this trauma. These are the most obvious kinds of bad fruit that come into our lives from this sin, or as God calls it abomination.

When we begin to stray from God, right and wrong become blurry. Life's choices are no longer black and white. Life's choices become more about whatever you feel is right is right. However, when God gave us guidelines to live by He made our lives good. He loves us. He is the only God that has a father's nature. He is the only God that truly loves us and wants the best for us. Any other god we serve will take life from us, and thereby destroy us.

God, What is My Baby's Name?

Chapter Eleven
Forgive and Live

I continued going to my weekly Bible study, learning more about God's love for me. Healed in my emotions and heart, my relationship with God as my Father and Lord, was becoming more intimate. I soon realized turning away from God, until I got answers for my aching heart, was selfish and immature. Yet God was very patient and longsuffering with me. Though it took time, He answered the questions I presented to Him. I now had every reason to live.

Through this difficult event in my life, I understood more about God's love for me. I understood that Jesus came so that we could live full lives. I understood that God was not the originator of sickness and death. I understood that scripture taught this was true.

When we don't have answers to our questions about why our loved ones die young, or why people suffer a long illness, we sometimes satisfy our hearts by justifying that this suffering is God's will. Often this blanket answer gives us some comfort in our time of loss. However, sickness and death are not God's will. Jesus came so we could enjoy abundant life. There was no sickness or death in the Garden of Eden before Adam and Eve sinned. Their world changed when they sinned.

When Jesus died on the cross, He destroyed all the works of darkness. He carried our sicknesses and grief in his own body on the cross. Isaiah addresses this.

> *But he was pierced for our transgressions,*
> *he was crushed for our iniquities, the*
> *punishment that brought us peace was on*
> *him, and by his wounds we are healed.*
> Isaiah 53:5, NIV

By receiving all that Jesus did for us, we can walk in a fullness of life. We can walk in health. If there is any problem a woman has during her pregnancy, she can ask God to heal her and the baby living inside of her.

When I read John 10:10 that day, I realized how much God loved me. He gave His only Son, Jesus to carry my sins in his own body to the cross and die for me. He paid a debt for me, that I could not pay. He sent the Holy Spirit to be with me, while I am here on earth.

Because of His sacrifice, I chose to forgive my doctors for encouraging me to have my baby in an abortion clinic. I chose to forgive my husband for not having the moral conscience to make a better decision other than abortion. I forgave my family for

Forgive and Live

not supporting me. I also forgave myself for making the wrong choice of abortion, even when I knew inside that it was the wrong thing to do.

When I forgave myself and others, it caused a healing to come to my heart. I felt released from the depression that existed earlier. He even told me the name of my baby as he is known in Heaven.

If you have had an abortion, you can receive forgiveness, and be healed of the negative effects it has had on you. You can forgive yourself and others around you. You can be free from the depression and the condemnation it has brought to your life.

I would like to pray with you, so you can be forgiven. Jesus already paid the price for your sins, all you have to do is tell him what you did wrong and ask Him to forgive you. He wants to heal you, so you can live. Pray this prayer with me.

Father, we come to You. You see everything, and know everything. I made the choice to have an abortion, and now I realize it was the wrong choice to make. I am so sorry that I did this. I ask You to forgive me for this. I ask that the blood of Jesus would wash me of this sin. I also want to forgive the doctors, and the nurses for what they did to my baby, and for the

God, What is My Baby's Name?

pain they caused me. I forgive my husband (or my boyfriend) for his involvement in this horrible decision that brought death to our child and that brought destruction into my life. I renounce all spirits of depression, murder, violence, anger, bitterness, suicide, hatred, idolatry, immorality, perversion, fear, death, and premature death that have been given access to me because of this act. I command them all to leave me now and never to return to me.

Mathew 18:18 says, "Truly I tell you, whatever you bind on earth will be bound in heaven, and whatever you loose on earth will be loosed in heaven." So I bind the demons of Molek, and command them all to leave me now.

I renounce and bind all other evil spirits that entered me during this abortion, and after this abortion. I command them all to leave me now. I close these doors now, and seal them with the blood of Jesus.

I declare that I am free of all condemnation,

and of all oppression, through the power of the blood of Jesus.

Thank you, Jesus, for paying the price for my sin with Your own blood. Thank You for forgiving me and for healing my body and making me whole again. I loose joy and peace in my life. Father, God I want Your will, and Your plans for my life. Amen!!

God, What is My Baby's Name?

More From the Author

A Baptism of Fiery Love is Coming

The Holy Spirit is at work in every person's life wooing and pursuing them to return to a loving relationship with Father God their Creator. This an individual process walked out by each person.

The Holy Spirit wants to introduce himself to each one of us. He came to heal our hearts and our bodies that we may have an abundant life and share in His glory. This is the beginning of an era of seeing and experiencing God's glory.

What Kind of Love is This?

With a burden to pray for the sick, Susan witnessed legs grow out, addictions leave, hips calcify causing patients to come off of long-term bed rest, and a dementia patient begin to have a clear mind. She learned the love of God through one miraculous encounter after another, including angels and divine intervention. Be empowered in the supernatural and receive an impartation for the miraculous love of God!

God, What is My Baby's Name?

Revealing God's Truth on Abortion

A Study Guide to *God, What is My Baby's Name?* "Whether you're a woman who has suffered in silence, a family member or friend with a loved one who has had an abortion, or a pastor or counselor, this book will provide insight, strategy and a practical process to restore hope and wholeness to broken lives."

—Jane Hamon

Five Smooth Stones to Slay Intimidation

God does not send us into battle without weapons. He has given us five smooth stones just like He gave to David to use against Goliath, the voice of intimidation that wants to rise up in our lives. We do not ever have to be intimidated or shut down again. Know your identity and authority God has given you. Walk in the love and grace from God that causes us to overcome all obstacles. Secure your smooth stone of humility that says, "I trust you Lord." With these five smooth stones in your sling of faith, you will slay the voice of intimidation in your life.

More from the Author

Stop Steven, Stop
. . . the angel yelled chasing after him

God does intervene in our lives and helps us and protects us from harm. He wants to be a Father to us and impart His love into us. The trauma of a child prematurely losing their life to alcohol or a chemical overdose is felt by many families. This can cause grief to weigh upon our hearts. It is through the Holy Spirit's comfort and being in a loving relational environment that heals the pain of a broken heart!

Restoring Your Heart

Susan Pender shares revelation that she received from God in a dream indicating wounds that needed to mend to restore her heart and soul. She relates her personal experience to the story of Nehemiah who was moved with compassion to assist the people to repair and rebuild the city walls and gates of Jerusalem. Susan shares how the Holy Spirit moved with compassion in her life to bring restoration to the shattered fragments of her heart and soul.

When someone is wounded by physical, mental, emotional, or sexual traumatic events, part of their heart and soul can separate from their whole personhood. These

God, What is My Baby's Name?

separated parts will hold the painful emotions associated with the traumatic memory. The more someone's heart and soul are harmed in this way, the more they become literally broken within.

We may not even be aware of the painful memory that caused the trauma, but the Holy Spirit knows everything about us and can help us bring restoration to our hearts and souls and wholeness to our lives. God sent His Son Jesus to earth to die for us and the Holy Spirit to help and comfort us to restore our hearts.

God uses the metaphor of a city to describe us.

> *The LORD is building up Jerusalem; He is gathering [together] the exiles of Israel. He heals the brokenhearted, And binds up their wounds [healing their pain and comforting their sorrow]."*
> Psalm 147:2, 3, AMP

The ruins and desolate places reveal areas that are broken within you. The exiles are all the broken pieces of your heart and soul that need to be healed and integrated back into their rightful places within you to make you whole again. God wants to restore the walls and gates of your life to make you strong in Him again.

For Speaking Engagements or Questions
Contact Susan Marie Pender

Susanmariepender@gmail.com
www.lilyofthevalleyhealing.com

www.ingramcontent.com/pod-product-compliance
Lightning Source LLC
Chambersburg PA
CBHW032213040426
42449CB00005B/574